A·FIRST·BOOK·OF SHAPES

Illustrated by David Anstey
Written by A J Wood

MODERN PUBLISHING
A Division of Unisystems, Inc.
New York, New York 10022

CIRCLE

SQUARE

TRIANGLE

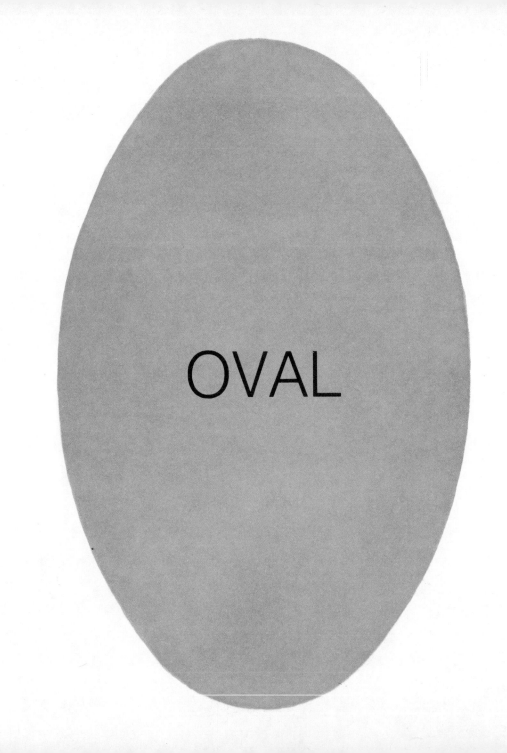

OVAL

RECTANGLE

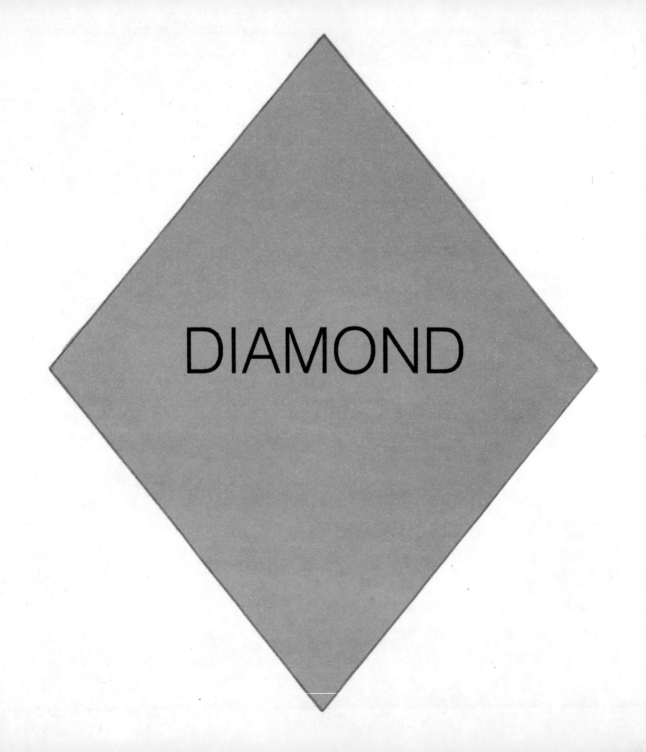

STAR

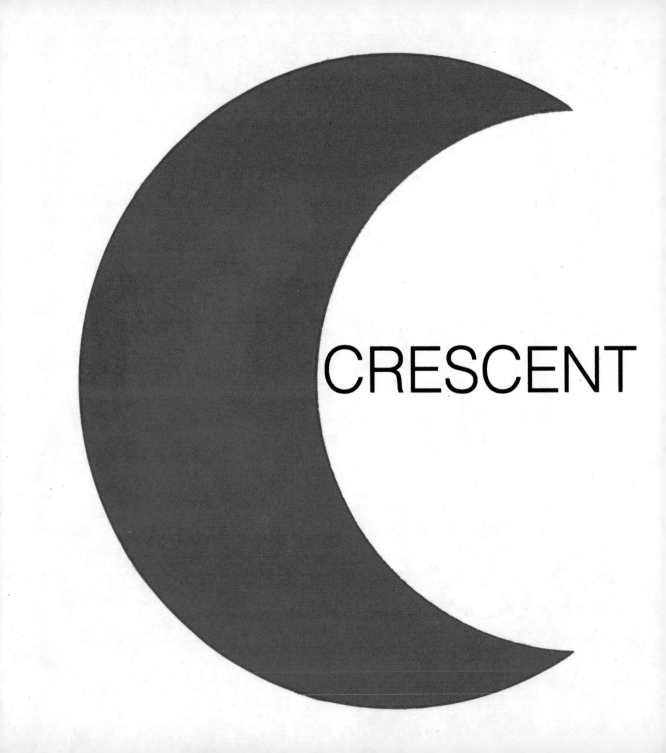

CRESCENT

Two triangles
can make...

...a diamond!

Two squares make...

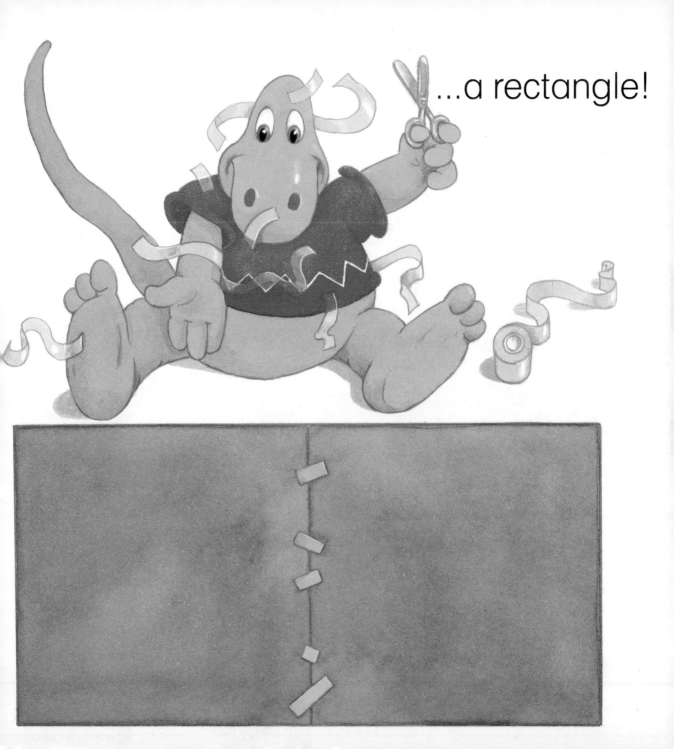

...a rectangle!

These objects are made up of different shapes.
How many can you see?

BUTTER[F]

HOUSE

BIRD

RABBIT

FLOWER   MUSHROOMS

FLOWER

INSECT

SNAIL

Look at these shapes again.
Point to each one and
say its name.

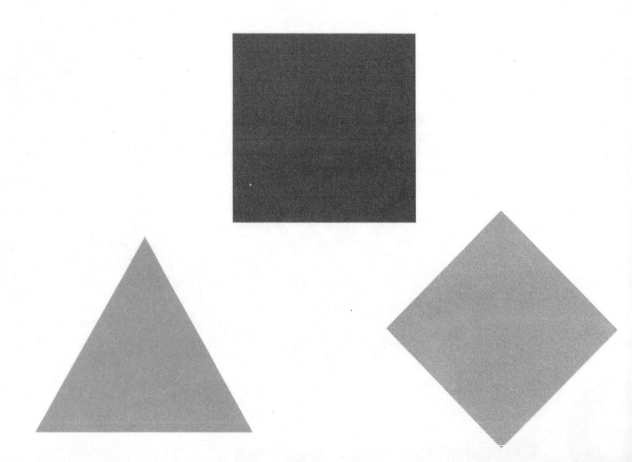